W9-BLT-383

THE ART OF
PAPER CUTTING

QUARRY

First published in the United States of America by
Quarry Books, a member of
Quayside Publishing Group
100 Cummings Center
Suite 406-L
Beverly, Massachusetts 01915-6101
Telephone: (978) 282-9590
Fax: (978) 283-2742
www.quarrybooks.com

ISBN-13: 978-1-59253-525-5
ISBN-10: 1-59253-525-9

10 9 8 7 6 5 4 3 2 1

Editor: Shoshana Brickman
Page Layout: Ariane Rybski
Photographs: Moshe Cohen

Printed in Singapore

BEVERLY MASSACHUSETTS

QUARRY BOOKS

THE ART OF
PAPER CUTTING

HENYA MELICHSON

Contents

Introduction

I ARRIVED AT THE ART OF PAPER CUTTING quite by chance, after having drawn, sketched, and painted for several years. After completing a few paper cuts, I became enchanted with the medium, as I realized that the skills I had been honing with pencils and paint could be expressed through paper cutting.

From that moment onward, I have been channeling my artistic efforts into paper cutting. With this book, I hope to convey that enthusiasm to you, and inspire you to find the same delight in this precise, ancient, and beautiful art.

The *Art of Paper Cutting* features a selection of paper cuts that I made over the course of several years, reflecting diverse influences in my life. In addition to calling upon styles and symbols traditionally used in paper cutting, I have also integrated artistic techniques usually associated with drawing to create works with depth and movement.

Some of the paper cuts communicate specific messages; others are simply aesthetic, designed for the purpose of expressing beauty. All of them have been done out of inspiration, love of the craft, and a belief that any imagined image can be created through paper cutting.

OPPOSITE, PARROT STAINED GLASS, BLACK PAPER WITH WHITE BACKING, 24" X 10" (61 X 25 CM)

✂ 7

PAPER CUTTING AROUND THE WORLD

Paper cutting is an ancient craft that is practiced in diverse forms in cultures around the world. In some cultures, only white and black papers are used; in others, colored papers and paints are favored. In some cultures, paper cuts are done only with scissors; in other cultures, sharp blades are used. In some cultures, the paper is folded once, twice, or several times before cutting; in other cultures, the paper is never folded.

Despite these differences, there are also many similarities. For example, paper cutting is generally connected to other arts, and may borrow ideas and patterns from other areas. In ancient China, paper cuts were used to transfer embroidery patterns, and for adding decorations to ceramics. Wood carvings had an impact on paper cutting in England, France, and Holland, while the patterns featured in Persian carpets inspired paper cutting for book covers in ancient Iran and Iraq. At the same time, diverse art forms have also been influenced by paper cutting. Lace patterns have been influenced by paper cut designs in Europe, the United States, and Mexico.

Asia

Paper cutting likely originated in China, the country where paper was invented. It is known here as jian zhi, and was traditionally used to transfer patterns, adorn walls and windows, and decorate presents. Chinese paper cuts are often cut from red paper; common motifs include flowers and animals.

In Japan, paper cutting is known as kirigami. A cousin of the widely known craft of origami (the art of paper folding), kirigami combines both folding and cutting. In ancient times, kirigami was used to cut the symbols of great Samurai families. Paper cut stencils were used to transfer these symbols to people's clothing and property.

Shadow puppetry is an Asian craft based on paper cutting. In these plays, puppets are cut from paper using sharp knives, and shows are carried out in front of an illuminated surface. These plays likely originated in China, but eventually spread throughout Asia, and are popular today in Thailand and India.

The Americas

The United States, as a center of immigrants, attracted people from all over Europe, and when they came, they brought with them distinct paper cutting traditions. Paper cuts were used for diverse purposes, including decorating religious texts, public documents, and cards. Traditional U.S paper cuts may depict homestead scenes or images associated with holidays. Paper cuts are particularly favored on Valentine's Day, when people often send frilly heart-shaped cards to their loved ones.

Mexico features a distinct form of paper cutting known as paper picado or punched paper. In this technique, artists use a hammer and chisel to punch designs onto stacks of thin colored paper. They may produce tens or hundreds of paper cuts at one time. The paper cuts are often cut into long banners, and used for decorations during Day of the Dead celebrations, and other holidays.

Europe

Paper cutting arrived in Europe during the fifteenth century, and was quickly embraced by craftspeople in several countries. Known as scherenschnitte in German, the craft became very popular in both Germany and Switzerland by the 1600s. It was used to cut stencils for furniture, embroidery, and lace patterns. One style that was particularly popular in these cultures was using paper cuts to decorate the front of greeting cards, while the inside featured a religious sign or the image of a saint. Another popular style, known as marques, involved cutting very delicate bookmarks. Paper cuts here are usually made with a blade, and the paper is not folded. Common motifs include mountain images, vases with flowers, rural scenes, and portraits.

In England, paper cutting became a pastime for people in the upper classes during the nineteenth century, alongside embroidery and other handicrafts. Silhouettes were a popular form of paper cutting all over Europe during the eighteenth and nineteenth centuries. They are an excellent method for reproducing the likeness of a person or place without using a camera.

In Holland, paper cutting is known as papiersnyden. It is traditionally done on white paper, without any addition of color. Dutch paper cuts are almost always cut with scissors, and though they may be either symmetrical or asymmetrical, the paper is almost always unfolded. One distinct Dutch style of paper cutting involves cutting small serrated scales.

In Poland, paper cutting is known as wycinanki, and dates to the nineteenth century. Polish paper cuts generally involve various colors of paper, often affixed in layers. These papers are cut, clipped, or torn, then assembled into a composite image. Peacocks, flowers, roosters, and star-shaped medallions are common motifs.

1

2

1 TRADITIONAL DUTCH PAPER CUT, RED PAPER ON WHITE BACKGROUND, 6" X 4" (15 X 10 CM)

2 TRADITIONAL POLISH PAPER CUT, BLACK PAPER WITH LAYERS OF COLORED PAPER ON WHITE BACKGROUND, 6" (15 CM) DIAMETER

Types of Paper Cuts

BOOKMARKS

Paper cuts can be used to fill a variety of functions, both practical and aesthetic. In the following pages, you will see examples of my favorite types of paper cuts, and get ideas on how you can put your own paper cuts to use.

If you are just starting out in paper cutting, bookmarks are excellent first projects. They are relatively small, which means you can likely complete one in just a few hours. Bookmarks aren't only for beginners, though, and you can integrate any type of design you like, be it simple, intricate, or something in between. Insert a piece of colored paper into a folded paper cut to add a colorful background to your design. Both functional and aesthetic, bookmarks make lovely gifts.

1

2

3

1 BIRD IN TREE BOOKMARK,
PINK PAPER ON PURPLE
BACKGROUND,
8" X 2½" (20 X 6 CM)

2 BUTTERFLIES BOOKMARK,
YELLOW PAPER ON BLUE
BACKGROUND,
8" X 2" (20 X 5 CM)

3 BIRDS AND TREES
BOOKMARK,
BLUE PAPER ON YELLOW
BACKGROUND,
8" X 2½" (20 X 6 CM)

DECORATIVE WALL HANGINGS

Paper cuts of any size can be mounted, framed, and hung on the wall. The subject of your paper cut may be anything under the sun, and use a range of colors. Paper cuts can be used to make blessings for the home, recreate a scene from a story, or convey meaning through the use of symbols and text.

1

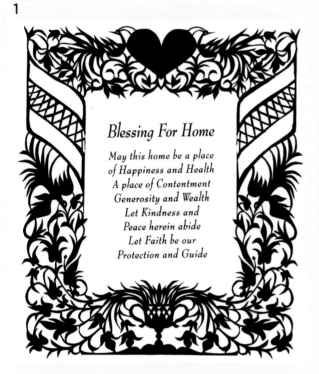

Blessing For Home

May this home be a place of Happiness and Health A place of Contentment Generosity and Wealth Let Kindness and Peace herein abide Let Faith be our Protection and Guide

2

1 GOD BLESS OUR HOME,
BLACK PAPER ON VARIEGATED
BACKGROUND,
3" x 8½" (8 X 22 CM)

2 A ROYAL WOMAN,
BLACK PAPER WITH GOLD
CELLOPHANE ON WHITE
BACKGROUND,
16" X 14" (41 X 36 CM)

FRAMES

Paper cuts can be excellent frames for mirrors, photographs, drawings, or paintings. Frames are often symmetrical and made with a vertical fold down the middle. Measure carefully before you begin cutting to make sure that the open area in the middle of the frame suits the object you are framing. In planning this type of paper cut, keep in mind that you want the paper cut to add beauty to the central object, but you don't want it to steal the show.

1

1 ROSE GARDEN FRAME,
BLACK PAPER ON MIRROR,
22" X 16" (56 X 41 CM)

GREETING CARDS

There are so many reasons to send greeting cards; making them yourself with paper cuts means you never have to rely on something from the store. You can make Christmas cards, New Year cards, Valentine's Day cards, birthday cards, or anniversary cards.

Paper cut designs are also excellent for making invitations—just bring your finished paper cut to a print shop and make high quality photocopies. Paper cuts made for this purpose can be mounted on metallic paper first, then onto card stock, for added festiveness.

1

2

3

4

1 SWAN GREETING CARD, WHITE PAPER ON VARIEGATED BACKGROUND, 7" X 4½" (18 X 11.5 CM)

2 LOVEBIRD CARD, CREAM PAPER ON VARIEGATED BACKGROUND, 7" X 4½" (18 X 11.5 CM)

3 CHRISTMAS CARD, BLUE PAPER ON VARIEGATED BACKGROUND, 7" X 4½" (18 X 11.5 CM)

4 PEACOCK WITH FLOWERS, ORANGE PAPER ON BLUE BACKGROUND, 4½" X 7" (11.5 X 18 CM)

Techniques

SYMMETRICAL

In symmetrical paper cuts, two sides of the paper cut are mirror images of each other. Paper cuts may be vertically or horizontally symmetrical, or both, depending on how they are folded. In these paper cuts, the paper is folded, and the design is drawn onto one side. The paper should stay folded until the entire paper cut is cut, since unfolding and refolding the paper can weaken the folded seam, and cause it to rip.

1

2

1 ANGELS WITH FLOWERS,
BLACK PAPER ON WHITE
BACKGROUND,
10" X 12" (25 X 31 CM)

2 DANCERS,
BLACK PAPER ON WHITE
BACKGROUND,
10" X 20" (25 X 51 CM)

3 HEART FILLED WITH LOVE,
BLACK PAPER WITH RED PAPER
ON WHITE BACKGROUND,
12" X 10" (31 X 25 CM)

01511 9811

ASYMMETRICAL

In asymmetrical paper cuts, the paper is not folded at all. The design is drawn onto the back of the paper before cutting.

1

2

3

1 INDIAN ELEPHANT,
BLACK PAPER ON WHITE
BACKGROUND,
10" X 8" (25 X 20 CM)

2 WOMAN IN LEAF,
BLACK PAPER ON WHITE
BACKGROUND,
12" X 8" (30 X 20 CM)

3 ANGEL WITH HARP,
BLACK PAPER ON WHITE
BACKGROUND,
8" X 6" (20 X 15 CM)

COMBINED SYMMETRICAL AND ASYMMETRICAL

Many of my paper cuts feature both symmetrical and asymmetrical elements. To make this type of paper cut, I draw and cut the symmetrical elements first. I already know how the asymmetrical elements will look, and usually sketch them on a piece of tracing paper in advance. I don't draw them on the paper cut until the symmetrical elements have been cut.

After cutting the symmetrical elements, I carefully unfold the paper cut and flatten the fold. Using the asymmetrical design that I sketched on the tracing paper as a guide, I sketch these elements onto the paper cut. When it comes to cutting the a symmetrical elements, I recommend using a knife rather than scissors, since using scissors at this stage can be tricky, and can cause the paper cut to rip.

1

2

1 WOMAN WITH CHILD,
BLACK PAPER ON WHITE
BACKGROUND,
12" X 8" (30 X 20 CM)

2 SCENES FROM THE CASTLE,
BLACK PAPER ON WHITE
BACKGROUND,
14" X 8" (36 X 20 CM)

POSITIVE

In positive cutting, elements of the design remain
in the paper, and the background is removed. For
example, if the paper cut is cut from white paper and
mounted on black paper, the white paper will feature
the design, and the black paper will show the background. In such paper cuts, all positive elements must
be connected; otherwise, they will fall out when the
background is removed.

NATURE'S LEAF,
BLACK PAPER ON WHITE
BACKGROUND,
12" X 8" (30 X 20 CM)

NEGATIVE

In negative cutting, elements of the design are cut out of the paper, and the background remains. For example, if the paper cut is cut from white paper and mounted on black paper, the white paper will show the background, and the black paper will feature the design.

A FAMILY TREE,
BLACK PAPER ON WHITE
BACKGROUND,
6" X 8" (15 X 20 CM)

COMBINED POSITIVE AND NEGATIVE

When starting out, it is easier to make the whole paper cut either positive or negative. However, as you gain experience, you'll find that combining the two cutting styles in a single design introduces a world of possibilities in terms of creating shade, movement, and three-dimensional effect.

This series of photos shows the steps in making Garden Boy. First, the image is drawn onto the back of silhouette paper and positive cutting is used to remove the background of the window areas **(1)**. After the windows are cut, I begin cutting other areas of the design **(2)**. I continue cutting the rest of the design. Note the mirror image of letters in the bottom right corner **(3)**. The finished paper cut is turned over and mounted on a white background **(4)**.

1

2

3

4

GARDEN BOY,
BLACK PAPER ON WHITE
BACKGROUND,
12" X 10" (30 X 25 CM)

Tools and Materials

Part of the universal appeal of paper cutting is that the supplies are inexpensive and very easy to find. All of the items below can be found in craft stores and online.

CELLOPHANE

This translucent, light material can be used to enhance your paper cut by adding a touch of delicate color. Cut the cellophane to size and affix behind your paper cut before mounting it on the desired background.

CUTTING MAT

You'll need one of these if you use a blade for paper cutting. I suggest selecting a self-healing mat, comprised of layers of PVC, since this type of mat won't disintegrate with use. Using this type of mat also reduces dulling of your blade. Make sure the cutting mat you use is a little larger than your paper cut.

CUTTING TOOLS

Paper cutting artists use either scissors or a blade to cut the paper. The choice is simply a matter of preference, so try your hand at both tools to determine which is most comfortable. Note that if you use a blade, you'll also need a cutting mat.

Scissors If you opt for scissors, choose a pair that is very sharp, and has short, straight blades. The shorter the blades on your scissors, the easier it is to make tiny and precise cuts.

Blade If you opt for a blade, choose one that is very sharp. I generally use a doctor's scalpel, but utility blades that can be sharpened or replaced easily are also excellent.

GLUE

Use acid-free white craft glue to affix colored paper, metallic paper, or cellophane to your paper cut, and to affix your paper cut to its background. Apply the glue in carefully placed dots; do not try to spread the glue, as this can cause the paper cut to tear.

LETTER AND PHRASE DECALS

Add a perfectly written personalized message to your paper cut using letter or phrase decals. Many companies sell phrases in prepared formats, and some even offer personalized phrases, allowing you to select the words, font, size, and color.

PAPER

Virtually any type of paper can be used for paper cutting, though you should keep in mind that the quality of the paper has a direct impact on the longevity of your work. At the same time, you don't want your paper to be too thick, since this can make cutting it more difficult. Here are some tips to keep in mind when selecting paper:

Cardboard or matboard This is the paper upon which you'll mount your paper cut when it is finished. Choose a color that harmonizes with the color of the paper cut.

Colored paper Polish-style paper cuts often feature several layers of brightly colored paper. Select colors that harmonize with each other and make sure that the paper isn't too thick, so that it doesn't bulge upwards from the papercut.

Metallic paper This type of paper can be used to make shimmering paper cuts, or to add a festive touch to a papercut cut from regular paper. If you are cutting the entire papercut from this paper, make sure it has a white or light-colored backing for drawing your design. Also, make sure the backing is well attached; otherwise, it can become separated from the metallic paper while you are cutting.

Silhouette paper This type of paper is black or dark-colored on one side, and white or light-colored on the other side. If you decide to make a dark-colored papercut, you'll need this type of paper, as the light-colored side provides the surface upon which you can draw.

Tracing paper or vellum This is perfect for making a preliminary sketch of your design. When you're happy with how the design looks on tracing paper, transfer it to the paper you'll be using for your papercut.

Variegated paper This type of paper features at least two colors that blend gradually from one to the next. When using it as a background for your papercut, consider the orientation of the paper before mounting the papercut.

White paper Most people start out using ordinary white paper (the type used in most home printers) for their paper cuts. I like to use slightly glossy paper, but paper with a matte finish is fine too. An advantage of using white paper is that you can add color to the final work if you like.

CUTTING MAT

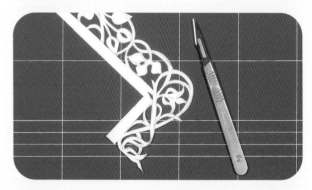

SCALPEL

CARDBOARD

SILHOUETTE PAPER

SKETCHING MATERIALS

You'll need a sharp pencil and eraser to draw your design onto the back of the paper. If you want straight lines or perfect circles, have a ruler and compass on hand, too.

WATERCOLORS AND FINE PAINTBRUSH

Painting your paper cut or its background adds artistic dimension. Be sure to use high quality watercolors that won't fade over time. Before applying the paint, test it on a piece of paper to make sure it isn't too wet. Overly wet paint can damage your paper cut.

WATERCOLORS AND FINE PAINTBRUSH

1

1 GOD BLESS OUR HOME,
BLACK PAPER ON VARIEGATED
BACKGROUND,
3" X 8¹/₂" (8 X 22 CM)

2 OPPOSITE, HEART IN
A WINDOW,
BLACK PAPER ON WHITE
BACKGROUND,
14" X 12" (36 X 30 CM)

2

From Imagination to Image

Paper cutting is a craft that requires careful planning and precise cutting. At the same time, it is also an art that can convey movement, flow, depth, and shadows. For me, paper cutting is akin to painting, only I use a sharp blade instead of a paintbrush. Even before I draw the initial outline for the design, I have arranged all the elements in my mind. Careful planning allows me to integrate winding branches, linked leaves, thoughtful owls, decorative ribbons, and other elements that give the work both spiritual meaning and visual harmony. After imagining the project completely, I carefully draw it onto the back of the paper. Though paper cuts are one-dimensional, I strive to create three-dimensional effects by combining negative and positive cutting techniques that create the impression of shadows and movement. Every detail of the image is drawn in advance, so that when I start cutting, I already have a very good idea of how it will look when it is finished. Below are some issues to consider as you plan your paper cut.

CENTER AND BORDER

In most of my paper cuts, the design is divided into a center and a border. The center usually features the main message or theme; the border generally features decorative elements, such as flowers, leaves, and wildlife, that complement the design, to enhance the meaning and complete the work. Motifs and symbols that appear in the center of paper cuts may include anything you like, including scenes from classical stories, words, messages, or symbols. The border of the paper cut may contain decorative elements such as vines, branches, flowers, text, or geometric shapes. Consider the following guidelines when designing your paper cut center and border:

- Take advantage of the border to express aesthetic elements. Integrate flowers, vines, animals, ribbons, geometric images, and whatever else you enjoy designing.
- Remember to use images that can connect elements from the center of the paper cut to its edges.
- In paper cuts that feature both symmetrical and asymmetrical elements, cut the symmetrical elements first.
- After you have unfolded the paper cut, sketch and then cut asymmetrical elements.

KEEP THINGS CONNECTED

When sketching the design on your paper cut, be sure that all of the elements are connected. This is necessary for making sure that none of the elements are left hanging (or fall out altogether) when the paper cut is finished. In some cases (when cutting text in negative, for example), you may need to make connections by integrating thin 'bridges' between the letters and the surrounding design. Adding vines, flowers, and leaves between objects is an excellent method of connecting the elements.

SYMBOLS

Integrating symbols into your paper cut design will imbue it with significance and meaning. At the right is a description of some of the symbols that appear in my paper cuts. Of course, you are free to integrate any symbols you like. Simply think about the function of your paper cut, and the message you want it to convey. I suggest conducting a little research about the symbols you want to use, as being informed about their meaning will make the paper cut even more meaningful.

BELLS
These delicate instruments can serve two functions. They can ring and make a beautiful sound when a gentle breeze passes by. They can also provide security, by ringing out a warning when evil spirits or dangerous winds blow by.

CHERUBS
These angelic figures bring to mind spirituality and youth. They are associated with both Christianity and Judaism, and are commonly used to decorate Valentine's Day cards, birthday cards, New Year cards, Christmas cards, etc.

FLOWERS, LEAVES, AND VINES
All the elements of your paper cut must be connected, and nature is an excellent source for making these connections. Consider adding winding vines, cascading flowers, and intricate leaves to your design. All of these motifs add beauty without detracting from the larger message.

GRAPES
A fruit favored by many artists, grapes and grape vines are symbols of renewal, joy, youth, and life. One of the seven plant species with which Israel was blessed in the Bible, grapes are used to make wine, a beverage that has religious significance in both Christianity and Judaism.

GRIFFINS
These legendary creatures are depicted with the head and wings of an eagle and the body of a lion. They are mentioned in Greek mythology, and were reputed to be trusted by the gods to protect their gold. Some scholars have even suggested that the griffin may be considered a cherub.

CHERUBS

LEAVES AND VINES

GRAPES

HAMSA

This five-fingered good luck charm image is common in both Middle Eastern and North African art, and is believed to stave off the evil eye.

HORN OF PLENTY

This image features a large horn filled with fruits, vegetables, and diverse vegetation. It is a symbol of abundance and wealth in diverse religions and regions.

OLIVES AND OLIVE BRANCHES

These are universal symbols of peace that date back to the biblical tale in which a dove brings an olive branch to Noah on his ark as a sign that the waters of the flood are receding.

POMEGRANATES

Since ancient times, these shapely red fruits have been valued for their medicinal qualities and durability. They are also admired for their large quantity of seeds, a trait which causes them to be associated with fertility. One of the seven plant species with which Israel was blessed in the Bible, it is believed that the number of seeds in a pomegranate is equal to the number of commandments in the Bible.

TREES

Whether it is a tree of life, a holiday tree, or an elegant weeping willow, trees lend themselves naturally to the art of paper cutting. Treetops are an excellent site for integrating symbols and hidden animals. Roots can be designed as intricately as you like, and are ideal for connecting elements in your paper cut.

HAMSA

HORN OF PLENTY

TREE

WILDLIFE

My paper cuts feature diverse animals and birds, including owls, elephants, deer, and peacocks. Before selecting an animal or bird for your design, consider its meaning and significance. Owls evoke wisdom; fish suggest fertility; roosters symbolize good luck; peacocks are associated with beauty; doves are connected with peace. Sketch the animal a few times in advance before drawing it onto your paper cut. Refer to photographs or other drawings for help.

TEXT

Integrating words and numbers into your paper cut gives it another dimension of meaning. For example, if your paper cut is meant to mark a wedding, anniversary, birthday, or other special occasion, you may want to include a special message. Areas with text are asymmetrical, so finish cutting all symmetrical elements before integrating text. To add text without cutting you can use decals. Simply plan the spacing of the letters in advance, or use prepared phrase decals. Some companies offer custom-made decals; simply order the message you want, in the size you want, and apply to your paper cut.

When writing a message that is to be cut into the paper cut, keep in mind that the mirror image of the message (and the letters) must be drawn on the back of the paper cut. I suggest practicing your message a few times on regular paper before transferring it to your paper cut.

As for the style of the letters, you may use an existing font, or draw the text freehand. Using an existing font has several advantages. There are plenty of choices available on most personal computers, and it is easy to select a font in the size and style you want. This ensures that all the letters match in style and size.

To prepare the letters, simply type the message into a regular word processing document on your computer, increase the font size as desired, and print. You may want to bold the text too, so that each letter is a little thicker. If you are designing your letters freehand, plan their spacing before drawing them, so that the spaces are even throughout the words. If your message requires more than one row of letters, leave a space that is double the height of your letters between the rows, so that the letters are easy to read. Decide whether you want to cut the letters in positive or negative. In positive letters, you remove the background; in negative letters, you remove the letters. If you are cutting positive letters, be sure to make bridges between the letters and the paper cut, so that the letters don't fall away after the background has been removed.

COLOR

Black paper cuts are often mounted on white backgrounds, and white paper cuts are often mounted on black backgrounds, because these colors contrast and create a clean impression, However, there is no reason not to experiment with other colors, thereby adding another dimension to your paper cut. Chinese paper cuts, for example, are often cut from red paper; in Mexico, paper cuts are usually made in a wide variety of bright colors.

Color can also be added after the paper cut has been cut. You can affix pieces of colored paper, metallic paper, or cellophane to the front or back of your paper cut. Color can also be added by painting the paper cut or the background.

KISS FOR A BIRD,
BLACK PAPER ON WHITE
BACKGROUND,
8" X 6" (20 X 15 CM)

Step-by-Step Instructions

In the following pages, you'll find step-by-step instructions and photographs for making two projects. Refer to these pages when cutting your first few paper cuts. See pages 115 to 128 for templates you can use to make your own paper cuts.

Tree and Rooster

12"X 8" (31 X 21 CM)

This symmetrical paper cut features two roosters facing each other below a stylized flower. The papercut is cut in positive using silhouette paper, and large areas of background are removed, meaning the backing you use will be quite visible. Use a white or variegated background for two quite different impressions. If you'd like to include a message in this papercut, the bottom strip is the perfect place for writing it.

✄ | TOOLS AND MATERIALS

- SILHOUETTE PAPER, 14" X 10" (36 X 25 CM)
- SKETCHING MATERIALS
- SCALPEL OR CUTTING TOOL
- SELF-HEALING CUTTING MAT
- GLUE
- WHITE OR VARIEGATED CARDBOARD, 12" X 8" (31 X 21 CM)

Tip   This is a positive design, which means you'll be removing the background. I suggest marking that part of the design with an X.

1

2

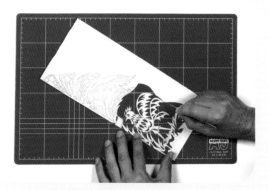

3

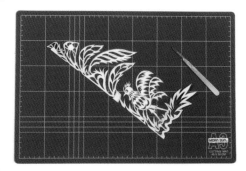

4

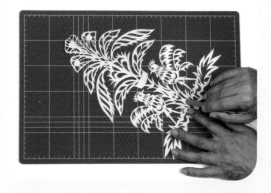

INSTRUCTIONS

1 Fold the paper in half lengthwise, so that the lighter side faces outward. Draw half of the design on one side, so that the middle of the design is along the fold.

2 Working in a systematic manner, start cutting the design. If you start at the top of the work, cut your way downward. Leave a border of paper around the entire paper cut to hold the paper cut together.

3 Cut the entire design, and remove all the background pieces.

4 Carefully unfold the paper cut, taking care that it doesn't rip as you separate the two sides. Press down on the back of the fold with your hand or the back of your cutting tool to flatten.

5 Mount the paper cut onto the desired background.

Heart of Love

10" X 9½" (26 X 24 CM)

This work features a symmetrical border and nonsymmetrical center. The border is drawn and cut first; the text in the center is drawn and cut afterward. The letters in this design are cut in negative. Make sure to include bridges when necessary so that the letters are not cut entirely from the paper cut. For example, when making the O, be sure to leave small bridges at the top and bottom of the letter, so that the center doesn't fall away.

Tip   Test paints on a piece of scrap paper before applying them to the papercut to make sure the paints aren't too wet.

1

3

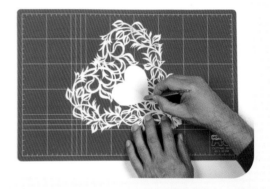

2

4

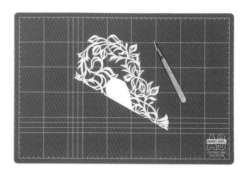

INSTRUCTIONS

1 Fold the paper in half lengthwise. Draw the symmetrical elements of the design on half of the paper, so that the middle of the design is along the fold. Leave an area in the middle of the design solid, as you'll be writing text here.

2 Working in a systematic manner, start cutting the design. If you start at the top of the work, cut your way downward. Leave a border of paper around the entire paper cut to hold the paper cut together.

3 Cut the entire design, and remove all the background pieces. Don't unfold the paper cut until you are completely finished cutting.

4 Carefully unfold the paper cut, taking care that it doesn't rip as you separate the two sides. Press down on the back of the fold with your hand or the back of your cutting tool to flatten.

5

7

6

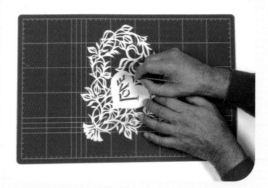

8

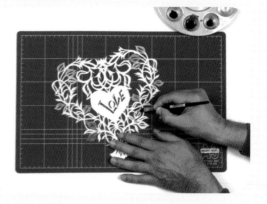

5 Lay the paper cut so that the back is facing upward, and write the mirror image of your text.

6 Cut out the letters.

7 Carefully remove the small pieces from the letters.

8 Paint as desired, then set aside to dry completely.

9 Mount the paper cut onto the cardboard.

Gallery of Projects

The following pages contain photographs, highlights, and instructions for more than 35 paper cut projects. Use these projects as inspiration and motivation for your own designs.

When selecting the paper for your paper cut, remember to give yourself a border of about 2" (5 cm) all around. Keep this border intact until you finish cutting the entire paper cut, as it provides stability during the cutting process.

BIRDS MEETING IN THE BARK

SQUIRREL ON A BRANCH

Holiday Tree

28" X 12" (71 X 30 CM)

This symmetrical design is cut from black paper, decorated with disks of gold, silver, and bronze metallic paper, and mounted on a white background. Most of the tree is cut in positive, although the base and bark feature a few negative elements.

This design features a tall, festive tree that narrows gently as it extends upward. Several pairs of birds are depicted in the tree, including two that are facing each other at the top. There is also a discreet pair of squirrels located on the second branch from the bottom, near the bark. To transform this festive tree into a family tree, simply cut out faces from family photographs and affix them instead of the metallic disks.

INSTRUCTIONS

1 Fold the paper in half lengthwise, so that the lighter side faces outward.

2 Draw half of the design on one side of the paper, so that the middle of the design is along the fold. Use a compass to draw several rounds hanging from the branches.

3 Cut the design in a systematic manner. Leave a border of paper holding the paper cut together until you finish cutting the design.

4 Carefully unfold the paper cut and flatten. Cut rounds of metallic paper and affix onto the rounds of the paper cut.

5 Mount the paper cut onto the cardboard.

✂ | TOOLS AND MATERIALS

- SILHOUETTE PAPER, 29" X 13" (74 X 33 CM)
- SKETCHING MATERIALS
- COMPASS OR SMALL ROUND OBJECT
- SCALPEL OR CUTTING TOOL
- SELF-HEALING CUTTING MAT
- METALLIC PAPERS, VARIOUS COLORS
- GLUE
- WHITE CARDBOARD, 30" X 14" (76 X 36 CM)

Tip This design features birds and squirrels that are "hidden" in the foliage. Draw these elements before drawing the leaves.

SMALL OWL NESTLED IN A FEATHER

Owls

19" X 10" (48 X 25 CM)

This asymmetrical design is cut from black paper and mounted on a white background. Most of the design is cut in positive. Notice that the claws on the tree stump are cut in negative, to contrast with the tree stump.

Owls are often associated with wisdom, and this owl certainly conveys a sense of insight and understanding. The owl is perched on a tree stump, and its eyes are looking directly forward. The body is comprised of several stylized feathers featuring a variety of cutting patterns. Some feathers depict leaves and branches. Some feathers feature delicate scales of the type typically used in Dutch paper cuts. One of the feathers features a small owl, looking directly outward just like the main owl, and explaining the plural title of this design. The tail is also comprised of several feathers. Each feather features diagonal lines that differ in width and angle.

INSTRUCTIONS

1 Draw the design on the lighter side of the paper.

2 Draw a smaller owl in one of the wings, positioning it at an angle that is similar to the large owl.

3 Cut the design in a systematic manner. Leave a border of paper holding the paper cut together until you finish cutting the design.

4 Carefully remove all the background pieces. Mount the paper cut onto the cardboard.

Tip This design features a variety of patterns on the body and wings. Practice a few patterns on a regular piece of paper before choosing the designs you like best.

THE FORBIDDEN FRUIT

AN EXOTIC BIRD

Eve's Seduction

5" X 20" (13 X 51 CM)

This asymmetrical design is cut from black paper and mounted on a white background. It is cut in positive, though the text featured in the snake's mouth—an excerpt from the Book of Genesis—is cut in negative.

This design is inspired by the biblical story of Adam and Eve in the Garden of Eden, with an important twist. The design depicts the body of a snake, which is divided into sections that illustrate several scenes from the story, as well as patterns that resemble snake scales and flowers. Eve is represented with long, flowing hair, but note that in this rendition of the story, she isn't tempted by a snake. Instead, it is an angel who offers her the forbidden fruit.

INSTRUCTIONS

1 Draw the design on the lighter side of the paper. Leave a solid area at the bottom of the mouth for writing the text.

2 Cut the design in a systematic manner, leaving a border of paper all around the snake.

3 On the lighter side of the paper, draw the mirror image of your text. Cut the text, and carefully remove all the background pieces.

4 Mount the paper cut onto the cardboard.

TOOLS AND MATERIALS

- SILHOUETTE PAPER, 7" X 22" (18 X 56 CM)
- SKETCHING MATERIALS
- SCALPEL OR CUTTING TOOL
- SELF-HEALING CUTTING MAT
- GLUE
- WHITE CARDBOARD, 7" X 22" (18 X 56 CM)

Tip

Practice writing the mirror-image text that appears on the bottom of the snake's mouth on a regular piece of paper before writing it on the paper cut.

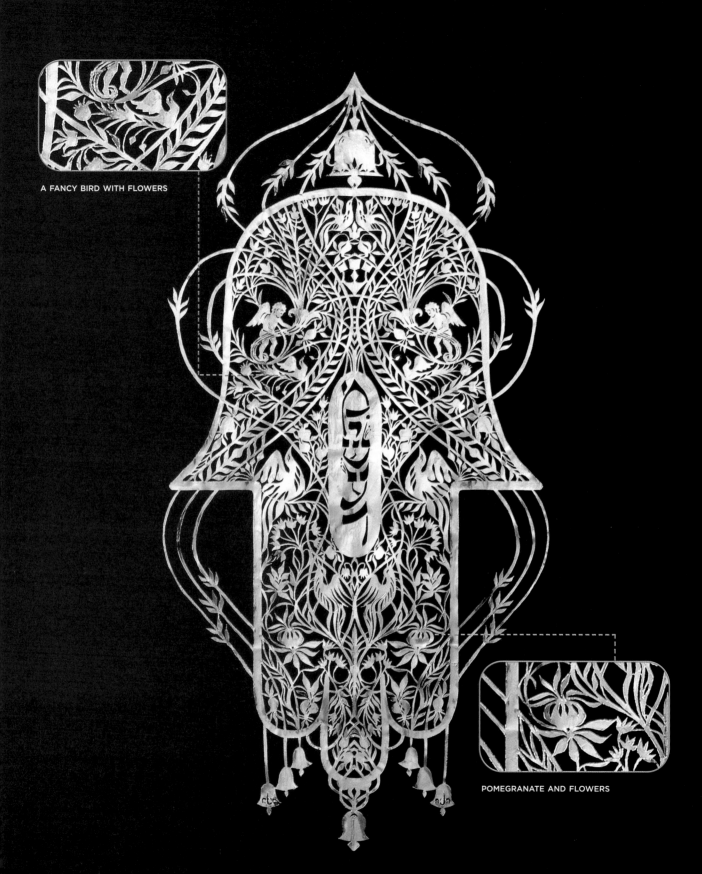

A FANCY BIRD WITH FLOWERS

POMEGRANATE AND FLOWERS

Golden Hamsa

27" X 13" (69 X 33 CM)

This mostly symmetrical design is cut from gold paper and mounted on a black background. The design is shaped like a hamsa, a symbol believed to bring prosperity and ward off evil. Most of the design is cut in positive, though the text in the center is cut in negative.

This paper cut is designed to protect a home, and features a number of elements that emphasize prosperity and protection. The use of gold paper suggests magnificence and wealth. Seven small bells are depicted at the bottom of the design, and one large bell is at the top. These bells are meant to ring should any bad spirits approach the house. As for the word in the center of the design, it means "from the gate," and was taken from a fourteenth century book of Kabbalah that was found in Syria.

INSTRUCTIONS

1 Fold the paper in half lengthwise, so that the lighter side faces outward.

2 Draw half of the design on one side, so that the middle of the design is along the fold. Leave a solid area in the middle of the design for writing the text.

3 Cut the design in a systematic manner. Leave a border of paper all around until you finish cutting the design.

4 Carefully unfold the paper cut and flatten. On the lighter side of the paper, draw the mirror image of your text, and cut. Mount the paper cut onto the cardboard.

Tip

Follow the wavy lines that extend upward from the small bells in this design, and you'll find that they meet at the top, right above the largest bell.

DETAILED LION'S MANE

Golden Lions

13" X 13" (33 X 33 CM)

This symmetrical design is cut from gold paper and mounted on a black background. A piece of pearl-colored cellophane is affixed at the middle of the design to accentuate the window.

The main image in this design is a pair of lions, facing each other. Lions symbolize wealth, monarchy, and majesty, elements that are enhanced by the use of gold paper. The general shape of the design is reminiscent of a crown, further contributing to this paper cut's majestic feel. The lions are positioned on a decorated wall-like background, with an elegant window at the top. Note the angled lines just above the lions' heads, giving the impression that the window actually sticks out from its background.

INSTRUCTIONS

1 Fold the paper in half lengthwise, so that the lighter side faces outward.

2 Draw half of the design on one side, so that the middle of the design is along the fold.

3 Cut the design in a systematic manner. Leave a border of paper all around until you finish cutting the design.

4 Carefully unfold the paper cut and flatten. Measure the cellophane and trim it so that it fits exactly behind the window.

5 Affix the cellophane to the back of the paper cut. Mount the paper cut onto the cardboard.

✂ | TOOLS AND MATERIALS

- METALLIC GOLD PAPER, 15" X 15" (38 X 38 CM)
- SKETCHING MATERIALS
- SCALPEL OR CUTTING TOOL
- SELF-HEALING CUTTING MAT
- GLUE
- PEARL-COLORED CELLOPHANE
- BLACK CARDBOARD, 15" X 15" (38 X 38 CM)

Tip This design is entirely symmetrical, so all of it can be drawn and cut while the paper is folded.

FISH WITH CAREFULLY CUT SCALES

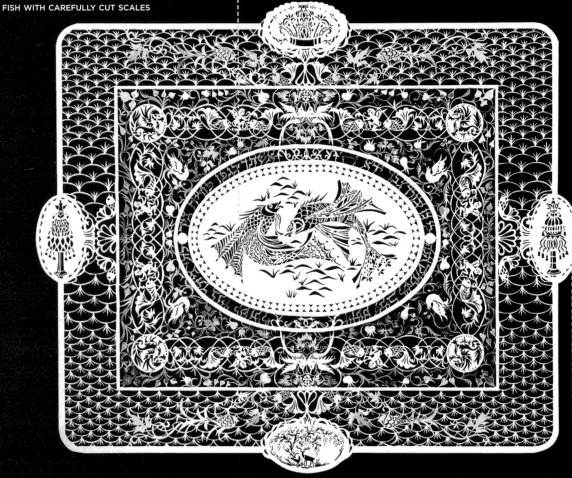

AN ELABORATE LAMP

Fertility Blessing

18" X 20" (46 X 51 CM)

This design features a mostly symmetrical border and an asymmetrical center. It is cut from white paper, painted with watercolors, and mounted on a black background.

The central symbol of this design is fish, signifying fertility and birth. The design is comprised of four areas. The main area is the oval shape located at the center of the piece. It features a pair of fish, cut in negative, and curved into one another. The next area features a blessing for the family from Psalm 128. The third area is a large rectangular shape surrounding the main pair of fish. This area is filled with images of angels, fish, pomegranates, and grapevines, and is cut in positive. The fourth area creates an impression of waves on the sea.

INSTRUCTIONS

1 Fold the paper in half lengthwise, then widthwise. Draw the symmetrical elements of the design.

2 Cut the design in a systematic manner. Leave a border of paper all around until you finish cutting the design.

3 Carefully unfold the paper cut and flatten. On the back of the paper, draw the asymmetrical elements, including the mirror-image text.

4 Cut the asymmetrical elements and the text. Paint as desired, then mount the paper cut onto the cardboard.

Tip

Practice writing the mirror-image text before writing it on the paper cut. The text is cut in positive, so be sure to include bridges that attach every letter to the paper cut.

FEATHERS MADE WITH
COLORED PAPER

A ROOSTER'S COLORFUL NECK

Colorful Tree

28" X 14" (71 X 36 CM)

This symmetrical design is cut from black paper, and mounted on a white background. Pieces of red, blue, yellow, and pink colored paper are layered and affixed on the front of the paper cut.

The design is inspired by traditional Polish paper cuts, which often feature several layers of colored paper. It features a large imaginary tree with four birds perched on its branches, and two birds standing at its base. Note that the tails of the birds in the branches blend into the edges of the tree. All the birds have vibrant tails and four of them have distinct crowns on their heads, reminiscent of peacocks or roosters.

INSTRUCTIONS

1 Fold the paper in half lengthwise, so that the lighter side faces outward.

2 Draw half of the design on one side, so that the middle of the design is along the fold.

3 Cut the design in a systematic manner. Leave a border of paper all around until you finish cutting the design.

4 Carefully unfold the paper cut. Cut pieces of colored paper that are slightly smaller than the uncut areas on the paper cut, and affix.

5 Mount the paper cut onto the cardboard.

Tip

Incorporate large solid areas in your design to give you the base for affixing layers of colored paper.

PRECISELY CUT FACIAL FEATURES

ROSE FABRIC BACKED WITH
CELLOPHANE

Woman in a Rose Dress

24" X 10" (61 X 25 CM)

This asymmetrical design is cut from black paper and mounted on a white background. Pieces of light purple cellophane are affixed to accentuate some folds in the skirt.

The design features a lovely woman standing in front of a stylized door. The woman is laden with jewelry, and dressed in an elegant gown that looks as if it were made from several different types of delicate materials. The dress was cut using very delicate cutting techniques in order to create the impression that it is cascading and flowing gently around the woman's body, imbuing the image with a sense of depth and movement.

INSTRUCTIONS

1 Draw the design on the lighter side of the paper. Cut the design in a systematic manner. Leave a border of paper all around until you finish cutting the design.

2 Select the areas of the dress that will be backed with cellophane, and trim the cellophane to size.

3 Affix the cellophane to the back of the paper cut. Mount the paper cut onto the cardboard.

✂ | TOOLS AND MATERIALS

- SILHOUETTE PAPER, 26" X 12" (66 X 30 CM)
- SKETCHING MATERIALS
- SCALPEL OR CUTTING TOOL
- SELF-HEALING CUTTING MAT
- LIGHT PURPLE CELLOPHANE
- GLUE
- WHITE CARDBOARD, 26" X 12" (66 X 30 CM)

Tip

The dress in this design is using a variety of very delicate cutting patterns, with the goal of creating the impression of movement and softness. Practice a few patterns on a regular piece of paper before choosing the patterns you like best.

ANGEL PLAYING WITH A HOOP

Playful Angels

15" X 10" (38 cm X 25 cm)

This symmetrical design is cut from black paper and mounted on a white background. It is cut almost entirely in positive and, as it is entirely symmetrical, all of it can be drawn and cut while the paper is folded.

The dominant shape in this design is the fanciful heart-shaped treetop that gives the entire paper cut a sense of happiness and cheerfulness. The treetop isn't just remarkable for its shape, however; take a close look at it and you'll see several creatures hidden amongst the leaves. The base of the tree is divided into two levels. The top level features two large angels and two large roosters; below this are two pairs of angels playing with toy hoops.

INSTRUCTIONS

1 Fold the paper in half lengthwise, so that the lighter side faces outward.

2 Draw half of the design on one side, so that the middle of the design is along the fold in the paper.

3 Cut the design in a systematic manner. Leave a border of paper all around until you finish cutting the design.

4 Carefully unfold the paper cut and flatten. Mount the paper cut onto the cardboard.

Tip

When drawing the treetop, draw the animals first, and then draw the leaves, so that the animals are discreetly concealed in the foliage.

BOWL OF GRAPES

HUNGRY BIRD

The Grape Harvest

15" X 15" (38 X 38 CM)

This design features a symmetrical frame and asymmetrical center. It is cut from black paper and mounted on a white background. A piece of purple cellophane is affixed in the top right area of the design to accentuate a window.

This design is a celebration of the grape harvest. It features two lovely maidens carrying baskets of freshly picked grapes. At the side is a young man playing the violin. The border is cut like a latticed fence, and features clusters of grapes and birds. The girls look as though they are chatting or giggling, and the lines of their skirts seem to swirl around their feet. The overall atmosphere is lighthearted and carefree.

INSTRUCTIONS

1 Fold the paper in half lengthwise, so that the lighter side faces outward.

2 Draw the symmetrical elements on one side, so that the middle of the design is along the fold.

3 Cut the design in a systematic manner. Leave a border of paper all around until you finish cutting the design.

4 Carefully unfold the paper cut. On the lighter side of the paper, draw the asymmetrical elements, and cut.

5 Measure the cellophane and trim it so that it fits exactly behind the window. Affix the cellophane to the back of the paper cut. Mount the paper cut onto the cardboard.

Tip The trellis-like border in this design features many straight lines. You can draw these freehand or use a ruler.

LEISURELY SNACK

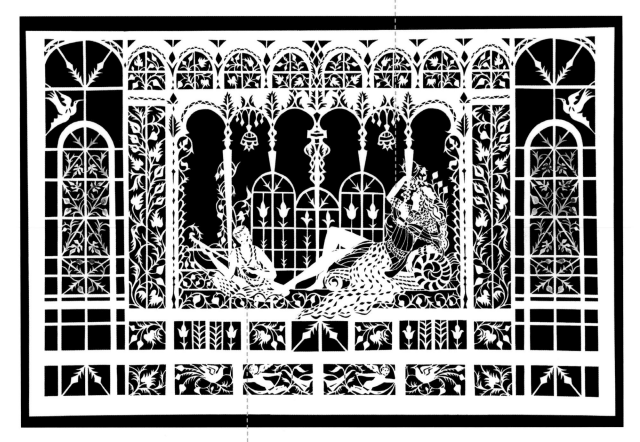

MUSICIAN PLAYS A TUNE

Woman and Musician

12" X 19" (30 X 48 cm)

This design features a symmetrical border and asymmetrical center. It is cut from white paper, selectively painted with watercolors, and mounted on a black background.

The design features a woman reclining in an elegant room that is surrounded by rich vegetation. The woman is wearing jewelry and elegant clothes; she seems to be completely relaxed as she nibbles on a bunch of grapes and listens to music being played for her pleasure by the musician positioned at the foot of her bed. The overwhelming sense of this design is one of peace, luxury, and tranquility.

INSTRUCTIONS

1 Fold the paper in half lengthwise.

2 Draw the symmetrical elements of the design on one side, so that the middle of the design is along the fold.

3 Cut the symmetrical elements in a systematic manner. Leave a border of paper all around until you finish cutting the design.

4 Carefully unfold the paper cut. On the lighter side of the paper, draw the asymmetrical elements, and cut.

5 Turn the paper over and paint as desired. Mount the paper cut onto the cardboard.

✂ | TOOLS AND MATERIALS

- WHITE PAPER, 14" X 21" (36 X 53 cm)
- SKETCHING MATERIALS
- SCALPEL OR CUTTING TOOL
- SELF-HEALING CUTTING MAT
- WATERCOLORS AND FINE PAINTBRUSH
- GLUE
- BLACK CARDBOARD, 14" X 21" (36 X 53 cm)

 Tip

Test paints on a piece of scrap paper before applying them to the paper cut to make sure the paints aren't too wet.

ANGEL GAZING OUTWARD

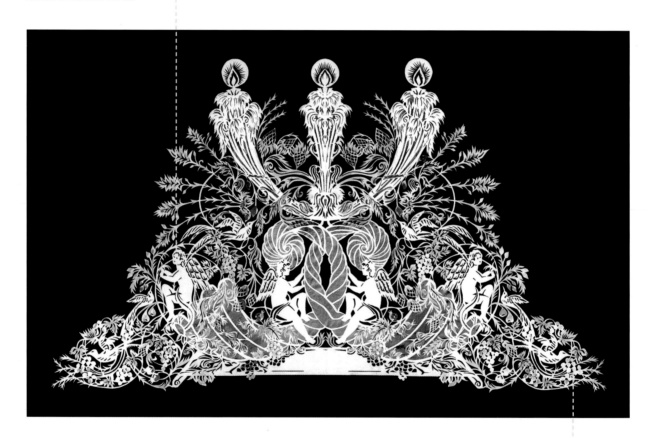

DELICATELY PERCHED BIRD

Three-Branched Candelabrum

13" X 14" (33 X 36 CM)

This symmetrical design is cut from white paper, painted with watercolors, and mounted on a black background.

The main element in this design is an elegant three-branched candelabrum, which holds three burning candles. The base of the candelabrum is made from two intertwined horns of plenty. Rich vegetation spills out the open end of each horn; the other end of the horn swirls into itself. There are two pairs of angels; one pair sits in the center of the candelabrum, facing each other and holding on to the horns of plenty; the other pair of angels faces outward. Sheaves of wheat, clusters of grapes, and diverse birds also appear in this design, contributing to the sense of richness and prosperity.

INSTRUCTIONS

1 Fold the paper in half lengthwise.

2 Draw half of the design on one side, so that the middle of the design is along the fold.

3 Cut the design in a systematic manner. Leave a border of paper all around until you finish cutting the design.

4 Carefully unfold the paper cut and flatten. Paint as desired, then mount the paper cut onto the cardboard.

✂ | TOOLS AND MATERIALS

- WHITE PAPER, 15" X 16" (38 X 41 CM)
- SKETCHING MATERIALS
- SCALPEL OR CUTTING TOOL
- SELF-HEALING CUTTING MAT
- WATERCOLORS AND FINE PAINTBRUSH
- GLUE
- BLACK CARDBOARD, 15" X 16" (38 X 41 CM)

Tip

This design is entirely symmetrical, so all of it can be drawn and cut while the paper is folded.

DEER FACING OUTWARD

WOMAN WITH FLOWERS IN HER HAIR

Woman at the Window

20" X 16" (51 X 41 CM)

This design features a symmetrical frame and asymmetrical center. It is cut from black paper and mounted on a white background. Elements of the background are painted with watercolors after the paper cut is mounted.

This design features a lovely young woman wearing many pieces of jewelry and sitting on a decorated window ledge. The ledge is covered with an elegant carpet, and surrounded by arches of vines and flowers. The landscape that is visible through the window features pine trees, gentle hills, and rocky walls. Watercolors were applied delicately after the paper cut was mounted onto the background to emphasize the landscape.

INSTRUCTIONS

1 Fold the paper in half lengthwise, so that the lighter side faces outward. Draw the symmetrical elements on one side, so that the middle of the design is along the fold.

2 Cut the design in a systematic manner. Leave a border of paper all around until you finish cutting the design. Carefully unfold the paper cut and flatten. On the lighter side of the paper, draw the asymmetrical elements, and cut.

3 Mount the paper cut onto the cardboard. Paint the landscape that is visible through the window.

✂ | TOOLS AND MATERIALS

- SILHOUETTE PAPER, 22" X 18" (56 X 46 CM)
- SKETCHING MATERIALS
- RULER
- COMPASS
- SCALPEL OR CUTTING TOOL
- SELF-HEALING CUTTING MAT
- GLUE
- WHITE CARDBOARD, 22" X 18" (56 X 46 CM)
- WATERCOLORS AND FINE PAINTBRUSH

Tip Make the designs in the arches as elaborate as you like by including elements such as birds, deer, elegant urns, and flowers.

Jerusalem

WINDOWS WITH DECORATIVE PANES

DELICATELY CUT FEATHERS

DISTINCTIVELY CURVED ROOFS

LAYERS OF BRICKS CUT IN POSITIVE

Jerusalem

18" X 25" (46 X 64 CM)

This design features a symmetrical border and asymmetrical center. It is cut in positive from silhouette paper and mounted on a white background.

The center of the design features several buildings in Jerusalem, many of them famous for their distinctive architectural style. I sketched these buildings during a visit to the city, but you can also use images from books and the Internet as models for drawing these buildings.

Interspersed among these structures are sentences from the Bible and poetic phrases connected with the city of Jerusalem. These passages are practical means of filling spaces between the buildings; they also imbue the work with a sense of poetry and music.

The buildings are surrounded by a frame comprised of stylized doves holding olive branches. Both the doves and the olive branches are associated with peace and prosperity, thus their presence blesses the city, and protects it. Note the detailed feathering of the doves, distinctive to Dutch paper cuts, and the stylized leaves at the bottom of the design.

Tip

The doves' wings make up the border of this artistic representation of Jerusalem. Be sure to leave yourself enough room between them for the images of the buildings.

OLD CITY'S WALL

THE CITY'S FAMOUS WINDMILL

CLASSIC-STLYE COLUMNS

DOME OF THE ROCK MOSQUE

INSTRUCTIONS

1 Fold the paper in half lengthwise, so that the lighter side faces outward.

2 Draw the symmetrical elements of the design on one side, so that the middle of the design is along the fold.

3 Cut the design in a systematic manner. Leave a border of paper all around until you finish cutting the design.

4 Carefully unfold the paper cut. On the lighter side of the paper, draw the asymmetrical elements and the mirror-image text.

5 Cut the asymmetrical elements and the text, and remove all the background pieces.

6 Mount the paper cut onto the cardboard.

(see picture on pages 64–65)

The Creation

CURVED LINES REPRESENT CLOUDS

BIRD AND SUN

STRAIGHT LINES DEPICT RAYS FROM
THE SUN

LEAVES AND GRASS

The Creation

16" X 26" (41 X 66 CM)

This majestic design is predominantly asymmetrical, although the columns along its left and right side are symmetrical. It is cut from black paper and mounted on a white background.

The inspiration for this design is the first passage the Bible: "In the beginning God created the heaven and the earth" (Genesis 1:1). The design is comprised of six sections. Two sections, the columns along the right and left, feature a pair of angels. The bottom angels are depicted blowing celebratory horns to declaration the creation. The other angels are present to protect the world from evil forces.

The center of the design is comprised of three ribbon-like strips that divide the main part of the design into four sections. The text on these strips, cut in negative, is taken from the Book of Genesis. As for the center of the design, it features elements associated with the natural world, including trees, flowers, and grass, the sun, the moon, stars, and clouds.

Notice that the order of these elements is not logical, as there are trees at both the top and bottom of the center, and the moon and sun are featured in the middle. Also notice the use of both negative and positive cutting techniques to depict the various elements. These techniques are used in order to represent the confusion and chaos that existed after the earth was created, as it is written in the second passage of the Bible: "Now the earth was unformed and void" (Genesis 1:2).

✂ | TOOLS AND MATERIALS

- SILHOUETTE PAPER, 18" X 28" (46 X 71 CM)
- SKETCHING MATERIALS
- RULER
- SCALPEL OR CUTTING TOOL
- SELF-HEALING CUTTING MAT
- GLUE

  WHITE CARDBOARD, 18" X 28" (46 X 71 CM)

Tip

In this design, the chaos of the biblical story is reflected in the positioning of the elements. For example, trees are located at the top and bottom of the design, while the moon and sun are in the middle.

ANGEL GAZING OUTWARD

DIVERSE CUTTING TECHNIQUE SHAPE A TREE BARK

ANGEL WITH TRUMPET

FLOWERS AND SUN RAYS

INSTRUCTIONS

1 Fold the paper in half lengthwise, so that the lighter side faces outward.

2 Use a ruler to mark the left and right borders of the design and draw the symmetrical elements.

3 Cut the symmetrical elements, then carefully unfold the paper cut. On the lighter side of the paper, draw three horizontal ribbons that divide this area into four sections. Draw the symmetrical elements and the mirror image of your text.

4 Cut the asymmetrical elements and the text.

5 Mount the paper cut onto the cardboard.

(see picture on pages 68–69)

LEAVES ON A DATE PALM TREE

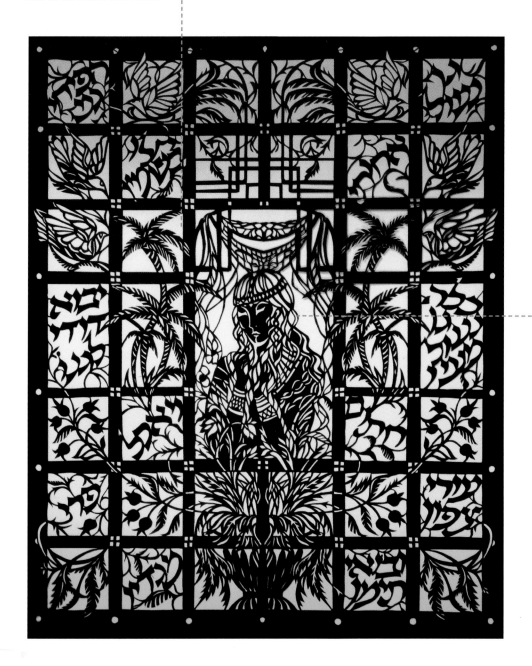

WOMAN GAZING DOWNWARD

Woman in the Garden

20" X 16" (51 X 41 CM)

This design features both symmetrical and asymmetrical elements. Though the border is primarily symmetrical, there are some places in which asymmetrical elements are incorporated. It is cut from navy blue paper, and mounted on a variegated background.

The design depicts a young woman sitting in the center of a large multi-paned window. The panes of the window look like bars, and there is a sense that the woman is trapped and cannot leave. The woman is looking downward, as though she is gazing outside the window; her head is slightly angled, as though she is listening to something—perhaps a song being played by her beloved? She is surrounded by palm trees, birds, and pomegranates, and an elegant vase is positioned just below her. The scene is inspired by the Song of Solomon 4:12: "A garden locked is my sister, my bride."

INSTRUCTIONS

1 Fold the paper in half lengthwise, so that the lighter side faces outward. Draw the symmetrical elements of the design, so that the middle of the design is along the fold. Use a ruler to make the straight lines of the window.

2 Cut the design in a systematic manner. Leave a border of paper all around until you finish cutting the design.

3 Carefully unfold the paper cut and flatten. On the lighter side of the paper, draw the asymmetrical elements, and cut. Orient the variegated cardboard as desired, and mount the paper cut on top.

Tip   When mounting your paper cut onto variegated paper, consider the orientation of the paper.

PROFILE OF A WOMAN

POMEGRANATES WITH BIRD

Profile with Grapes

16" X 16" (41 X 41 CM)

This design features both symmetrical and asymmetrical elements. It is cut from white paper, painted with watercolors, and mounted on a black background.

This design features many pomegranates and grapevines, two symbols that relate to prosperity. The center of the design is the profile of a young woman whose hair is comprised of lush vegetation that sits like a crown upon her head. Two young musicians are depicted just below the profile, and birds are featured throughout the design. The overall impression of this design is of life, beauty, and renewal.

INSTRUCTIONS

1 Fold the paper in half lengthwise.

2 Draw the symmetrical elements of the design on one side, so that the middle of the design is along the fold. Leave a semicircular area in the middle solid for drawing the profile.

3 Cut the design in a systematic manner. Leave a border of paper all around until you finish cutting the design.

4 Carefully unfold the paper cut. On the back of the paper cut, draw the asymmetrical elements, and cut.

5 Paint as desired. Mount the paper cut onto the cardboard.

Tip You may want to use a compass to draw the circular area that frames the face in the middle of the design.

BIRDS MEET IN THE MIDDLE

PROFILES IN AN EMBRACE

Lovers

20" X 16" (51 X 41 CM)

✂ | TOOLS AND MATERIALS

- SILHOUETTE PAPER, 22" X 18" (56 X 46 CM)
- SKETCHING MATERIALS
- SCALPEL OR CUTTING TOOL
- SELF-HEALING CUTTING MAT
- GLUE
- VARIEGATED CARDBOARD, 22" X 18" (56 X 46 CM)

This design features a symmetrical border and asymmetrical center. It is cut from navy blue paper and mounted on a variegated background. It features both negative and positive cutting.

The central image in this design is a pair of lovers sitting in a gentle embrace in front of a decorated lattice. The couple is positioned inside a window that is surrounded with rose vines. Images of roses are featured below the lovers as well, enhancing the sense of love, romance, and elegance. Two elegant vases are positioned on either side of the couple, and extending from these vases is an arc of lush and beautiful vegetation. The vegetation meets at the top of the design, in the image of two birds meeting beak to beak, as if in a kiss. Note that the vases, flowers, and birds that comprise the top area of the border are cut in negative, and the strips of roses at the bottom, as well as the couple in the middle, are cut in positive.

INSTRUCTIONS

1 Fold the paper in half lengthwise, so that the lighter side faces outward. Draw the symmetrical elements on one side, so that the middle of the design is along the fold in the paper.

2 Cut the symmetrical elements in a systematic manner. Leave a border of paper all around until you finish cutting the design.

3 Carefully unfold the paper cut and flatten. On the lighter side of the paper, draw the asymmetrical design, and cut. Orient the variegated cardboard as desired, and mount the paper cut on top.

Tip   Consider using a painting or photograph for inspiration and guidance when drawing your design.

JESTER PATS A PEACOCK

JESTER WATCHES A BIRD FLY

Court Jesters

26" X 10" (66 X 25 cm)

This symmetrical design is cut from black paper and mounted on a white background. Pieces of orange and red cellophane are affixed at the back of the paper cut, giving it the appearance of stained glass.

This design is divided into six parts that are cut to resemble real windows. The top and bottom windows feature jesters such as those that may be seen in traditional Italian theater. The jesters at the top are sitting with peacocks, while those at the bottom look upward toward two flying birds. The window is surrounded by leaves and flowers. The jesters and windows are cut in positive, while the trim around the design is cut in negative.

INSTRUCTIONS

1 Fold the paper in half lengthwise, so that the lighter side faces outward.

2 Draw half of the design on one side of the paper, so that the middle of the design is along the fold.

3 Cut the design in a systematic manner. Leave a border of paper all around until you finish cutting the design.

4 Carefully unfold the paper cut and flatten. Measure the red and yellow cellophane and trim it to size.

5 Affix the cellophane to the back of the paper cut. Mount the paper cut onto the cardboard.

- SILHOUETTE PAPER, 28" X 12" (71 X 30 cm)
- SKETCHING MATERIALS
- RULER
- COMPASS OR ROUND OBJECT
- SCALPEL OR CUTTING TOOL
- SELF-HEALING CUTTING MAT
- GLUE
- RED AND YELLOW CELLOPHANE
- WHITE CARDBOARD, 28" X 12" (71 X 30 cm)

Tip This design features horizontal and vertical lines, several circles, and rounded arches. You may want to use a ruler and compass to draw these elements precisely.

ANGEL GOING UPWARD

JACOB SLEEPS ON A ROCK

Jacob's Ladder

20" X 14" (51 X 36 CM)

This design features a symmetrical border and asymmetrical center. It is cut from black paper and mounted on a white background.

The design is inspired by the biblical story of Jacob's ladder, as recounted in Genesis 28. Jacob is on a long journey, weary and exhausted, he chooses a rock in the desert upon which to lay his head. While sleeping, he dreams of a ladder reaching up to the sky upon which angels ascend and descend. In this design, Jacob is depicted in flowing robes and sandals, lying on the ground with a rock as his pillow. A winding ladder extends toward the sky, and on that ladder are several angels. Some of the angels are facing Jacob, thus descending, while others face the heavens, thus ascending. Palm trees in the background evoke the desert in which Jacob slept. As for the border, it contains several lyres, as well as decorative columns, flowers, and leaves.

INSTRUCTIONS

1 Fold the paper in half lengthwise, so that the lighter side faces outward.

2 Draw the symmetrical elements on one side, so that the middle of the design is along the fold.

3 Cut the design in a systematic manner. Leave a border of paper all around until you finish cutting the design.

4 Carefully unfold the paper cut. On the lighter side of the paper, draw the asymmetrical elements, and cut. Mount the paper cut onto the cardboard.

Tip The coat Jacob is wearing in this design is inspired by the so-called coat of many colors that Jacob wears in the biblical story.

BIRD FLYING DOWNWARD

ANGEL LOOKING UPWARD

Angel Holding a Candelabrum

16" X 12" (41 X 30 CM)

This design features a symmetrical top and asymmetrical bottom. It is cut from black paper and mounted on a white background.

The center of this design features an angel who is holding a decorated candelabrum. The top of the candelabrum features nine candle cups, plus two birds on either side. Both the top and bottom of this candelabrum are made up of grapes and grape leaves. Note that these elements are symmetrical at the top and asymmetrical at the bottom.

INSTRUCTIONS

1 Fold the paper in half lengthwise, so that the lighter side faces outward.

2 Draw the symmetrical elements of the design on one side, so that the middle of the design is along the fold.

3 Cut the symmetrical elements in a systematic manner. Leave a border of paper all around until you finish cutting the design.

4 Carefully unfold the paper cut. On the lighter side of the paper, draw the asymmetrical design, and cut. Mount the paper cut onto the cardboard.

Tip

Note that in this design, the top is symmetrical and the bottom is asymmetrical.

PROFILE OF WOMAN LOOKING DOWNWARD

BOY OFFERS A BIRD

The Gift

16" X 14" (41 X 36 CM)

This design features a symmetrical border and asymmetrical center. It is cut from black paper and mounted on a white background.

The center of this design features an elegant woman receiving a bird from a young boy. A stylized tree is positioned behind the woman, and its branches hang gracefully above her. This area is cut in negative, enabling the fine details of the leaves and the woman's dress to be expressed, and creating an effect that is almost two-dimensional, so that one feels the movement in these elements. As for the border, this is the area in which the design really opens up. It is cut in positive, with thin lines and large spaces that give a sense of lightness that contrasts with the darker center.

INSTRUCTIONS

1 Fold the paper in half lengthwise, so that the lighter side faces outward.

2 Draw the symmetrical elements of the design on one side, so that the middle of the design is along the fold.

3 Cut the design in a systematic manner. Leave a border of paper all around until you finish cutting the design.

4 Carefully unfold the paper cut and flatten. On the lighter side of the paper, draw the asymmetrical elements, and cut.

5 Mount the paper cut onto the cardboard.

Tip Note how the leaves on the tree and the woman's dress are cut in a manner that suggests movement and flow.

PAINTED PINK FLOWER

PROFILE OF A BIRD

Stained Glass Birds

28" X 16" (71 X 41 CM)

This symmetrical design is cut from black paper and mounted on a white background. The background is painted with watercolors.

The paper cut, designed to resemble a real window, is comprised of several small panes. A large symmetrical flower sits at the top of the windows, and there are two smaller flowers at either side. Below these flowers are two colorful birds that meet beak to beak. The birds have elaborate tails that reach the bottom of the paper cut, where they intertwine with flowers and leaves.

INSTRUCTIONS

1 Fold the paper in half lengthwise, so that the lighter side faces outward.

2 Draw half of the design on one side, so that the middle of the design is along the fold. Use a ruler to make the straight lines.

3 Cut the design in a systematic manner. Leave a border of paper all around until you finish cutting the design.

4 Carefully unfold the paper cut and flatten. Mount the paper cut onto the cardboard and paint the background as desired.

Tip

Take advantage of the large white background areas in this design to enhance the design with watercolors.

PROFILE OF A BIRD

DEER DEPICTED IN POSITIVE AND NEGATIVE

Wall Candlesticks

20" X 12" (51 X 30 CM)

This symmetrical design is cut from black paper and mounted on a white background.

The design features an elaborate wall candelabrum comprised of various animal and floral shapes. At the top of the candelabrum, positioned as though they are protecting everything below, is a pair of griffins. Under the griffins is an oval-shaped area, which features two deer that seem to be entering a gated area. The deer, cut in both positive and negative, are surrounded by leaves and floral elements. Below this area is a small five-branched candelabrum. The bottom of the design is filled with lush vegetation of leaves and flowers. There are pairs of birds on either side, and above each pair of birds is an angel supporting a candle.

INSTRUCTIONS

1 Fold the paper in half lengthwise, so that the lighter side faces outward.

2 Draw half of the design on one side, so that the middle of the design is along the fold.

3 Cut the design in a systematic manner. Leave a border of paper all around until you finish cutting the design.

4 Carefully unfold the paper cut and flatten. Mount the paper cut onto the cardboard.

Tip This design is entirely symmetrical, so all of it can be drawn and cut while the paper is folded.

TWO BIRDS MEET AT THE TOP

LEAVES IN THE MIDDLE

Birds of Love

12" X 11" (30 X 28 CM)

This symmetrical design is cut from black paper and mounted on a white background. Pieces of red, orange, and yellow cellophane are affixed, often in layers.

The design is inspired by traditional Polish paper cuts. It features three hearts in the center, two of which are decorated with colored paper, and one of which features an intricate design of leaves. These hearts are surrounded by two flowery branches that form another heart around them. There are pairs of birds at the top and bottom of the design.

INSTRUCTIONS

1 Fold the paper in half lengthwise, so that the lighter side faces outwards.

2 Draw half of the design on one side, so that the middle of the design is along the fold.

3 Cut the design in a systematic manner. Leave a border of paper all around until you finish cutting the design. Make sure you incorporate large solid areas in your design. You'll need these for affixing the colored papers.

4 Carefully unfold the paper cut and flatten. Cut pieces of colored paper that are smaller than the uncut areas on your paper cut and affix.

5 Mount the paper cut onto the cardboard.

Tip The order of the colored papers in this design is always the same, with yellow papers cut in the largest size, and affixed directly onto the paper cut. These are topped with smaller pieces of red and orange paper.

A BASKET OF FLOWERS

BOY SMELLING A FLOWER

Women and Children

20" X 16" (51 X 41 cm)

This symmetrical design is cut from black paper and mounted on a variegated background. Note that the bottom area of the design is both vertically and horizontally symmetrical.

This design is divided into two sections. The top section depicts two women and two children who have gone to the garden to pick flowers. The women are wearing elegant flowing dresses; each one holds a basket that is overflowing with flowers, and offers the child flowers to smell. The two sides of this section are divided by a classic Greek-style vase. The bottom section features four pairs of birds.

INSTRUCTIONS

1 Fold the paper in half lengthwise, so that the lighter side faces outward. Fold the bottom third of the paper in half upward.

2 Draw half of the design on one side, so that the middle of the design is along the middle fold.

3 Cut the design in a systematic manner. Leave a border of paper all around until you finish cutting the design.

4 Carefully unfold the paper cut and flatten. Orient the variegated cardboard so that the darker area is at the bottom, and mount the paper cut on top.

Tip Note that birds depicted on the bottom area of the design will appear four times rather than twice, due to the additional fold.

WOMAN REACHING UP TO A BIRD

TROUBADOUR PLAYS A FLUTE

The Troubadours

10" X 20" (25 X 51 CM)

This symmetrical design is cut from black paper and mounted on a white background. It is cut almost entirely in positive though some elements are depicted in negative.

The design features a scene in which two young women are sitting, with birds perched on their hands, inside an elegant room with decorated windows and wall. Two troubadours are located at either end of the room. They are standing under arched openings and playing their instruments, likely for the listening pleasure of the women. Note the landscape that is featured outside the openings where the troubadours are playing. The background buildings and trees are cut in very small dimensions to create an effect of depth and distance.

INSTRUCTIONS

1 Fold the paper in half lengthwise, so that the lighter side faces outwards.

2 Draw half of the design on one side, so that the middle of the design is along the fold.

3 Cut the design in a systematic manner. Leave a border of paper all around until you finish cutting the design.

4 Carefully unfold the paper cut and flatten. Mount the paper cut onto the cardboard.

Tip Though most of this design is cut in positive, some elements (such as the chandeliers) are cut in negative to make it more interesting.

PEACOCK WATCHING THE PLAYERS

PLAYER LEANING ON A TREE

Players Under a Tree

13" X 12" (33 X 30 cm)

This symmetrical design is cut from black paper and mounted on a white background.

It depicts a pair of players sitting in tranquility under the shade of a tree and playing music. A pair of elegant birds serves as their audience. Though the entire design is cut in positive, note how the wide open spaces of the background contrast with the dark solidity of the bark and the players' legs. As for the birds, note how their head feathers extend and become integrated into the background.

INSTRUCTIONS

1 Fold the paper in half lengthwise, so that the lighter side faces outward.

2 Draw half of the design on one side, so that the middle of the design is along the fold.

3 Cut the design in a systematic manner. Leave a border of paper all around until you finish cutting the design.

4 Carefully unfold the paper cut and flatten. Mount the paper cut onto the cardboard.

✂ | TOOLS AND MATERIALS

- SILHOUETTE PAPER, 15" X 14" (38 X 36 cm)
- SKETCHING MATERIALS
- SCALPEL OR CUTTING TOOL
- SELF-HEALING CUTTING MAT
- GLUE
- WHITE CARDBOARD, 15" X 14" (38 X 36 cm)

Tip

Take advantage of the branches and leaves in this tree to create an interesting abstract design, if you like.

THE FAMOUS FIDDLE

CHIMNEY AND SHINGLES

Fiddler on the Roof

12" X 9" (30 X 23 CM)

This asymmetrical design is cut from black paper and mounted on a white background. It is cut entirely in negative.

The design is based on a scene from Fiddler on the Roof, the widely loved tale written by Sholem Aleichem. The tale was made into a musical, and has been produced on stages around the world for the past 40 years. This paper cut, designed to look like a drawing of a scene from the play, features a fiddler on his roof, looking up towards the heavens.

INSTRUCTIONS

1 Draw the design on the lighter side of the paper.

2 Cut the design. Be sure to leave bridges of paper between all of the elements in the design.

3 Mount the design onto the cardboard.

✂ | TOOLS AND MATERIALS

- SILHOUETTE PAPER, 14" X 11" (36 X 28 CM)
- SKETCHING MATERIALS
- SCALPEL OR CUTTING TOOL
- SELF-HEALING CUTTING MAT
- GLUE
- WHITE CARDBOARD, 14" X 11" (36 X 28 CM)

Tip   When recreating scenes from plays or stories, be sure to choose elements that are easily recognizable.

THREE BIRDS MEET IN THE MIDDLE

WOMAN GAZES AT A BIRD

The Bird Woman

20" X 15" (51 X 38 CM)

This design features a symmetrical border and asymmetrical center. It is cut from black paper and mounted on a blue background. Pieces of glossy blue paper are affixed at the back of the design.

The focus of the design is a woman enjoying the company of birds. Several elaborate birds stand in front of her, and their feathers seem to merge with her skirt. There is a bird perched on her hand, and several more flying over her head. On either side of the woman are two columns deigned in a classic architectural style. The columns are decorated with ribbons, grapes, and birds. Above the woman is a decorated gable featuring symbols that represent wealth and prosperity, including clusters of grapes and horns of plenty. At the base of each column is a lion, symbolizing majesty and glory.

INSTRUCTIONS

1 Fold the paper in half lengthwise, so that the lighter side faces outward. Draw the symmetrical elements of the design on one side, so that the middle of the design is along the fold.

2 Cut the symmetrical elements in a systematic manner, then carefully unfold the paper cut. On the lighter side of the paper, draw the asymmetrical design, and cut.

3 Decide which areas you want to highlight and cut the blue paper to size. Affix the blue paper on the back of the paper cut. Mount the paper cut onto the cardboard.

Tip   In this paper cut, blue paper is used as a backing for the center of the paper cut, and certain elements of the border. This helps connect the two areas, bringing them together with a splash of color.

AN ANGEL LOOKING
INWARD

FLAME BURNS AND CANDLE
MELTS

Pair of Candlesticks

16" X 8" (41 X 20 CM)

This symmetrical design is cut from black paper and mounted on a white background.

This design features a pair of candlesticks that resemble ancient columns. A lace cloth is depicted at the base of the candlesticks, and the wavy pattern of the cloth contrasts with the vertical lines of the candlesticks. At the top of each candlestick is a Hellenistic-style pot within which candles are positioned. A pair of angels is perched on each candlestick, wrapping the candlesticks in ribbons.

INSTRUCTIONS

1 Fold the paper in half lengthwise, so that the lighter side faces outward.

2 Draw half of the design on one side, so that the middle of the design is along the fold.

3 Cut the design in a systematic manner. Leave a border of paper all around until you finish cutting the design.

4 Carefully unfold the paper cut and flatten. Mount the paper cut onto the cardboard.

Tip   You may want to use a ruler to make the lines in the candlesticks as straight as possible.

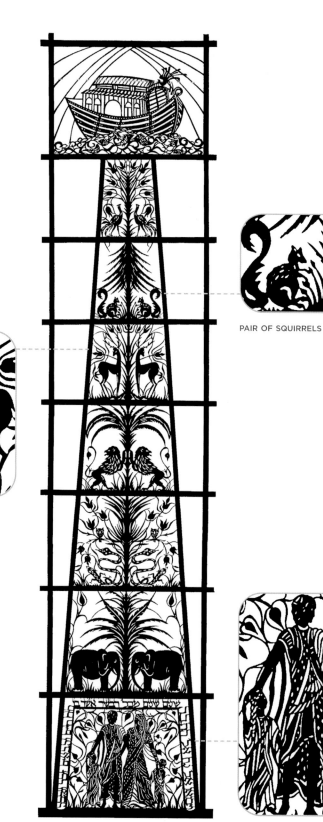

PAIR OF DEER

PAIR OF SQUIRRELS

NOAH AND HIS FAMILY

Noah's Ark

44" X 16" (112 X 41 CM)

This design is predominantly symmetrical, though the top and bottom images of the ark and Noah's family are asymmetrical. It is cut from black paper and mounted on a white background.

The design is based on the biblical story of Noah's ark, as told in Genesis 6–9, in which God punished the world for its sins by causing a great flood. God felt Noah was the only righteous person left on earth, and commanded him to build a giant ark so that he and his family could escape the flood. God also told Noah to bring pairs of every creature on earth into his ark, in order to save them from the flood. This famous ark is featured at the top of this design, on a stormy sea that is filled with fish. Below this are seven levels, arranged like a ladder. The bottom level features Noah and his family; above them are pairs of animals including elephants, snakes, lions, deer, squirrels, and peacocks, as well as lush vegetation.

INSTRUCTIONS

1 Fold the paper in half lengthwise, so that the lighter side faces outward.

2 Use a ruler to divide your design into eight sections. Draw half of the middle six designs, so that the middle of the designs are along the fold.

3 Cut the symmetrical elements in a systematic manner. Be sure to leave the ladder-like border all around.

4 Carefully unfold the paper cut. Draw the asymmetrical images at the top and bottom of the design, and cut. Mount the paper cut onto the cardboard.

Tip
Take a look at the story of Noah's ark before drawing your design, and include images from the story that are most interesting to you.

BIRD WITH ELEGANT FEATHERS

FLOWERS, BERRIES, AND LEAVES

Butterflies

13" X 14" (33 X 36 CM)

This symmetrical design is cut from black paper and mounted on a white background. It is cut in positive.

The title of the design is Butterflies, in the plural form, and if you look closely, you will see several little butterflies concealed in the wings of the main butterfly. In addition to these little butterflies, the wings also contain flowers, leaves, and birds. These images were chosen as they represent the butterfly's natural surroundings, thus the butterfly and its environment are presented in a single unified image.

INSTRUCTIONS

1 Fold the paper in half lengthwise, so that the lighter side faces outward.

2 Draw half of the design on one side, so that the middle of the design is along the fold.

3 Cut the design in a systematic manner. Leave a border of paper all around until you finish cutting the design.

4 Carefully unfold the paper cut and flatten. Mount the paper cut onto the cardboard.

Tip This design features decorated circles on every wing, much like a real butterfly. You may want to use a compass to draw these circles.

MYTHIC GRIFFINS ADD PROTECTION

BELLS ADD MUSIC AND PROTECTION

The Artist at Work

11" X 19" (28 X 48 CM)

This symmetrical design is cut from navy blue paper and mounted on a variegated background. It frames a photograph of me at work, and features protective symbols and images.

The design is divided into three sections. The main section holds the photograph, which is guarded on either side by a pair of griffins. Around these griffins is a profusion of rich vegetation, adding natural beauty and life to the design. The vegetation sprouts from two large classic jugs situated on either side of the photograph. Below the photograph and griffins are two rows of small arches. There is a bell inside each arch, and one above the photograph as well. These bells contribute both to the beauty and security of the design. Their purpose is twofold: When they ring, they bring musical pleasure. They can also ring when bad winds are near, in order to warn people of a visiting bad spirit, or to scare off evil spirits.

INSTRUCTIONS

1 Fold the paper in half lengthwise, so that the lighter side faces outward. Mark a framed area where the photograph will be placed, and draw the paper cut design all around it.

2 Cut the design in a systematic manner. Leave a border of paper all around until you finish cutting the design.

3 Carefully unfold the paper cut. Affix the photograph behind the framed area at the center of the paper cut. Mount the paper cut onto the cardboard.

Tip The framed area in this paper cut is rectangular, but you can also make a round picture frame in the center. Just use a compass to mark the frame.

BIRDS MEET IN THE MIDDLE

Love
is a bridge
between two
Hearts

DELICATE PAINTING ADD BEAUTY

Painted Heart

7" X 8" (18 X 20 cm)

This symmetrical design is cut from white paper, painted with watercolors, and mounted on a black background.

The paper cut features several elements traditionally associated with love, including lush, colorful flowers and a pair of lovebirds. The center of the heart is an ideal place for writing a message. It can be used as a Valentine's Day card, anniversary card, wedding card, or simply to say "I love you".

INSTRUCTIONS

1 Fold the paper in half lengthwise.

2 Draw half of the design on one side, so that the middle of the design is along the fold. Be sure to make a large open area in the middle of the design for text.

3 Cut the design in a systematic manner. Leave a border of paper all around until you finish cutting the design.

4 Carefully unfold the paper cut and flatten. Paint as desired and set aside to dry. Mount the paper cut on the black cardboard.

5 Write message in center of paper cut using letter or phrase decals.

✂ | TOOLS AND MATERIALS

- WHITE PAPER, 9" X 10" (23 X 25 cm)
- SKETCHING MATERIALS
- SCALPEL OR CUTTING TOOL
- SELF-HEALING CUTTING MAT
- WATERCOLORS AND PAINTBRUSH
- GLUE
- BLACK CARDBOARD, 9" X 10" (23 X 25 cm)
- LETTER OR PHRASE DECALS

Tip

Plan the layout of your message carefully so that the letters are balanced and tidy. You may want to apply the decals before mounting your paper cut.

WATER LILY

WOMAN BRAIDING HER HAIR

Woman and Water Lilies

14" X 19" (36 X 48 CM)

This asymmetrical design is cut from black paper and mounted on a variegated background. It features a combination of positive and negative cutting techniques.

The main image of this design is a young woman, braiding her hair while she sits atop a water lily. Most of the woman is cut in positive, though the part of her body that overlaps with the moon is cut in negative. The background is airy and open, because of the use of thin lines and large, wave-shaped spaces. The waves are cut in different sizes to create a sense of movement.

INSTRUCTIONS

1 Draw the design on the lighter side of the paper.

2 Cut the design in a systematic manner, leaving a border of paper to hold the paper cut together.

3 Orient the variegated cardboard so that the lighter end is at the top, and mount the paper cut onto the cardboard.

Tip

When mounting your paper cut onto variegated paper, consider the orientation of the paper. In this design, placing the darker end of the paper at the bottom suggests the depth of the water.

ABOUT THE AUTHOR

Henya Melichson has been a paper cut artist for more than twenty years. With a background in painting and drawing, Henya's paper cuts are inspired by various sources, including religious and secular motifs, ethnic images and traditions, poetry, and nature. Her works have been exhibited in museums in Europe, the United States, and Israel. She has held several solo exhibitions, including one in the Openbare Bibliotheek in Amsterdam, Holland. She has also participated in group exhibitions in the United States and Europe, including a show at the Knipselmuseum in Westrbork, Holland. Henya is a member of the Guild of American Paper cutters, and has led seminars, instructed paper cutters, and been interviewed for television programs.

Templates

In the following pages, you'll find more than a dozen templates you can use to make your own paper cuts. Simply photocopy the template (this option allows you to increase the size with ease), or trace it onto tracing paper. Transfer the design to the paper you'll be using for your paper cut. Copy the Xs onto your paper as well, because these are the areas that will be cut away from the paper cut.

If the template you are using is half of a symmetrical design, or if you'd like the design to appear on both sides of the paper, line up the dotted edge of the template with the fold in your paper when copying the design.

SYMMETRICAL DEER AND TREE FRAME

SYMMETRICAL BIRDS AND LEAF FRAME

SYMMETRICAL ANGEL FRAME

SYMMETRICAL HEART-SHAPED FLORAL FRAME

SYMMETRICAL POMEGRANATE AND JUG FRAME

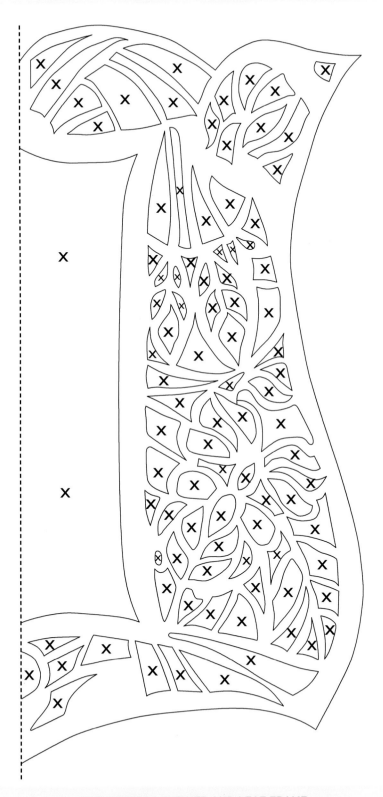

SYMMETRICAL FLOWER AND LEAF FRAME

BIRD GREETING CARD

BIRD WITH ROSE GREETING CARD

ANGEL WITH HORN GREETING CARD

SYMMETRICAL FESTIVE TREE

SYMMETRICAL JUG WITH FLOWERS

SYMMETRICAL HEART WITH FLOWERS AND BIRDS

FLORAL BOOKMARK